GRATEFUL DEAD
FOR UKULELE

ISBN 978-1-4950-0701-9

HAL•LEONARD®
CORPORATION

7777 W. BLUEMOUND RD. P.O. BOX 13819 MILWAUKEE, WI 53213

For all works contained herein:
Unauthorized copying, arranging, adapting, recording, Internet posting, public performance,
or other distribution of the printed music in this publication is an infringement of copyright.
Infringers are liable under the law.

Visit Hal Leonard Online at
www.halleonard.com

CONTENTS

Althea

Words by Robert Hunter
Music by Jerry Garcia

First note

Verse
Moderate, laid-back feel

1. I told Al - the - a   I was   feel - in' lost,
2.–4. *See additional lyrics*

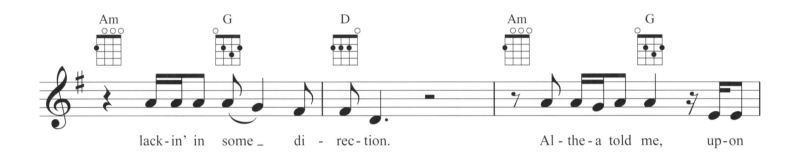

lack - in' in some _ di - rec - tion.   Al - the - a told me,   up - on

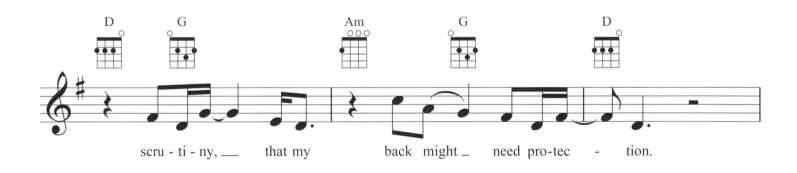

scru - ti - ny, __ that my   back might _ need pro - tec - tion.

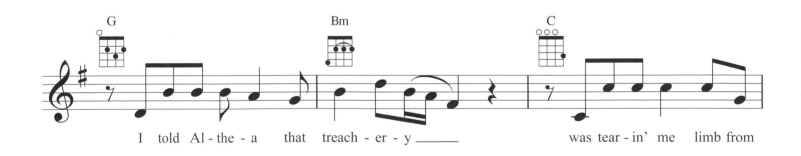

I told Al - the - a   that treach - er - y _____   was tear - in' me limb from

Copyright © 1980 ICE NINE PUBLISHING CO., INC.
All Rights Administered by UNIVERSAL MUSIC CORP.
All Rights Reserved   Used by Permission

limb. Al - the - a told me, "Now, cool down, boy. _

Set - tle back; _ eas - y, Jim." __

To Coda ⊕

1., 2.

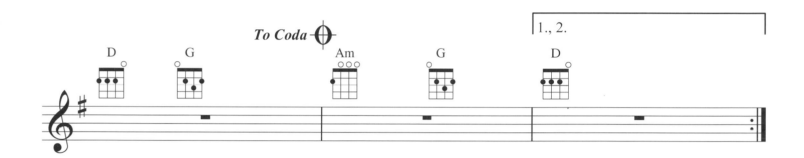

3.

Bridge

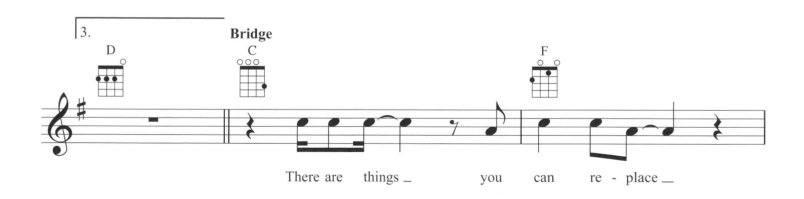

There are things _ you can re - place __

and oth - ers you ____ can - not. ____

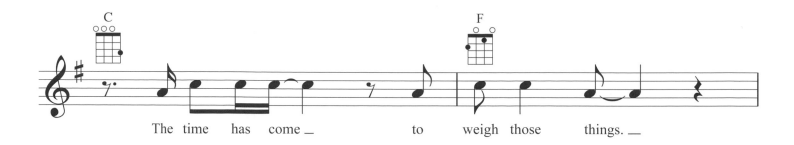

The time has come __ to weigh those things. __

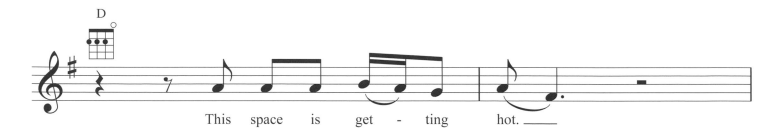

This space is get - ting hot. _____

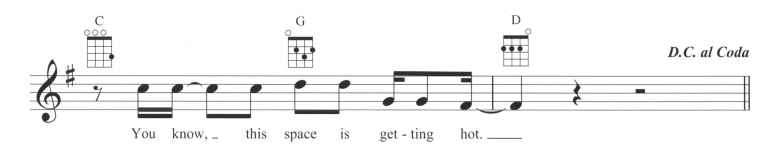

D.C. al Coda

You know, _ this space is get - ting hot. _____

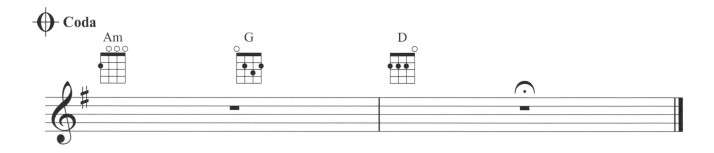

⊕ Coda

Additional Lyrics

2. You may be Saturday's child all grown,
Moving with a pinch of grace.
You may be a clown in the burying ground
Or just another pretty face.
You may be the fate of Ophelia,
Sleeping and perchance to dream,
Honest to the point of recklessness,
Self-centered to the extreme.

3. Ain't nobody messin' with you but you.
Your friends are getting most concerned.
Loose with the truth, maybe it's your fire,
But, baby, don't get burned.
When the smoke has cleared, she said,
That's what she said to me:
You're gonna want a bed to lay your head
And a little sympathy.

4. I told Althea I'm a roving sign,
That I was born to be a bachelor.
Althea told me, "Ok, that's fine."
So now I'm out trying to catch her.
I can't talk to you without talking to me.
We're guilty of the same old thing,
Thinking a lot about less and less
And forgetting the love we bring.

Bird Song

Words by Robert Hunter
Music by Jerry Garcia

First note

Verse
Moderately slow, in 2

1., 3. All I know __ is, some - thing like a bird __
2. When you hear __ that same __ sweet song a - gain, __

__ with - in __ her sang. __
__ will you __ know why? __

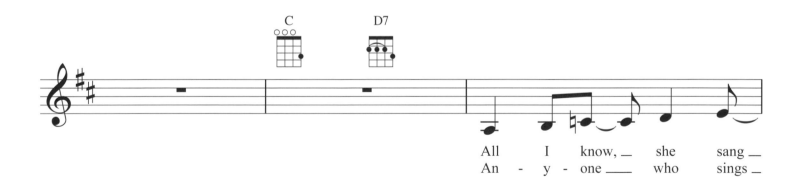

All I know, __ she sang __
An - y - one __ who sings __

__ a lit - tle while __ and then __ flew __ on. __
__ a tune so sweet __ is pass - ing __ by. __

Copyright © 1971 ICE NINE PUBLISHING CO., INC.
Copyright Renewed
All Rights Administered by UNIVERSAL MUSIC CORP.
All Rights Reserved   Used by Permission

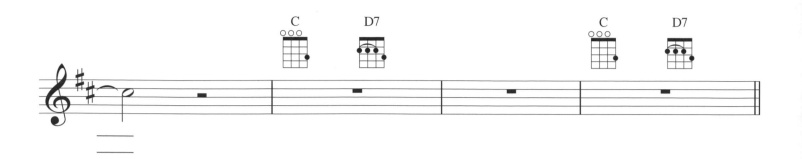

Chorus

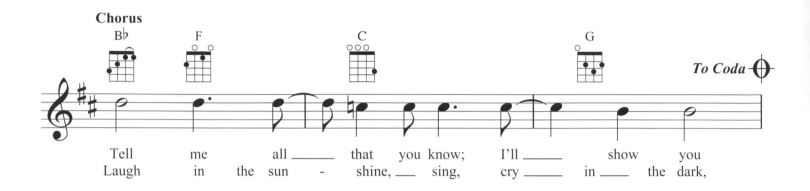

Tell   me   all ____ that   you   know;   I'll ____ show   you
Laugh   in   the   sun - shine, __ sing,   cry ____ in ____ the   dark,

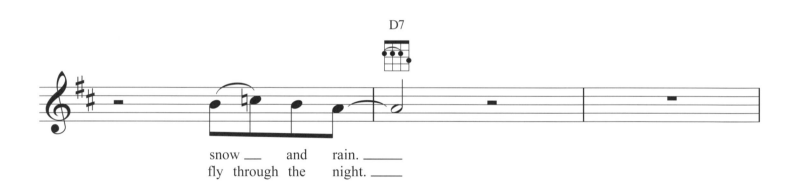

snow __ and   rain. _____
fly through the   night. _____

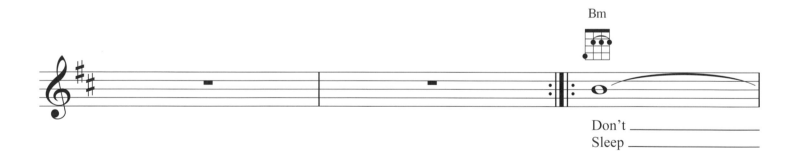

Don't _____
Sleep _____

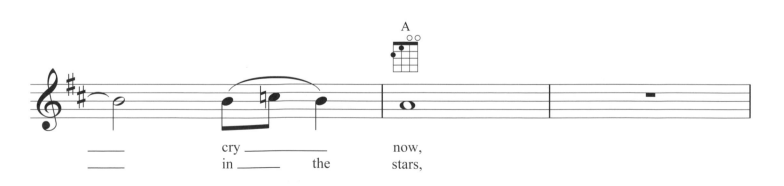

____ cry _____ now,
____ in _____ the   stars,

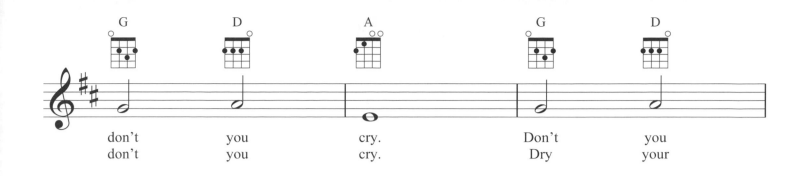

don't you cry. Don't you
don't you cry. Dry your

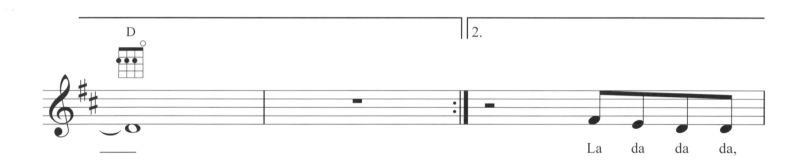

cry an - y - more. _____ La da da da. _____
eyes on _____ the wind. _____

1.

2.

_____ La da da da,

D.C. al Coda
(Lyric 1)

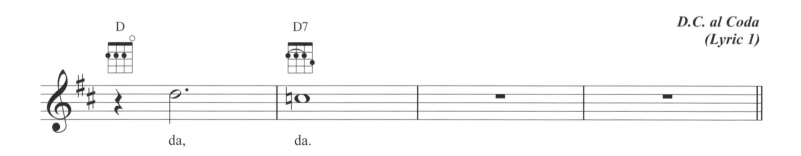

da, da.

Coda

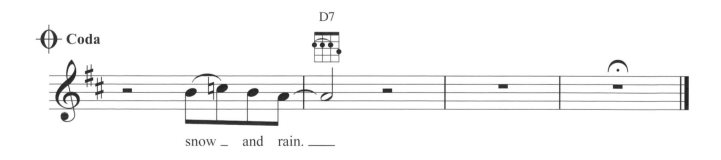

snow _ and rain. _____

Box of Rain

Words by Robert Hunter
Music by Phil Lesh

First note

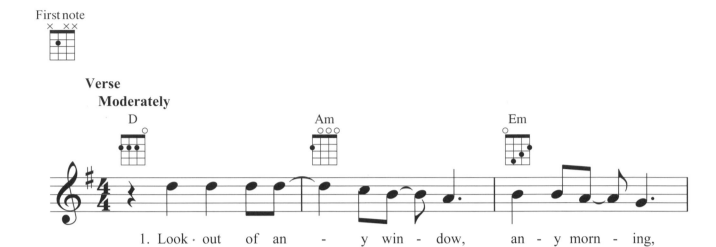

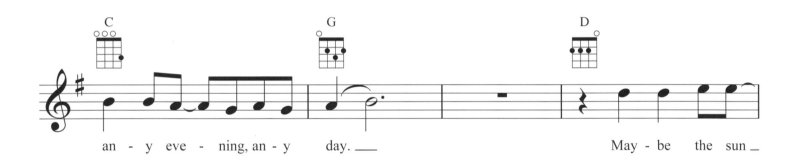

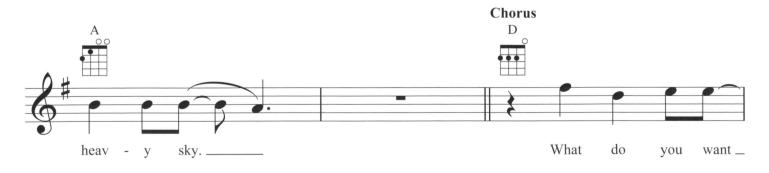

Copyright © 1970 ICE NINE PUBLISHING CO., INC.
Copyright Renewed
All Rights Administered by UNIVERSAL MUSIC CORP.
All Rights Reserved   Used by Permission

Verse

4. Walk in - to splin - tered sun - light, inch your way — through dead — dreams to an - oth - er land. _____ May - be — you're tired — and bro - ken, your tongue is twist - ed with words half spo - ken and

Chorus

thoughts un - clear. _____ What do you want — me to — do, — to do — for — you _____ to see — you through? _____ A box of rain — will

Outro

Brokedown Palace

Words by Robert Hunter
Music by Jerry Garcia

Copyright © 1971 ICE NINE PUBLISHING CO., INC.
Copyright Renewed
All Rights Administered by UNIVERSAL MUSIC CORP.
All Rights Reserved   Used by Permission

pal-ace on my hands and my knees. ___ I will roll, ___ roll, roll. ___

___ Make my-self a bed ___ by the wa - ter - side, ___

___ in my time, in my time, ___ I will roll, ___ roll, roll. ___

Chorus

___ In a bed, ___ in a bed, ___ by the wa - ter - side ___ I will

lay ___ my head. Lis - ten to the riv - er sing ___ sweet songs ___ to

1., 2.

rock my soul. ___

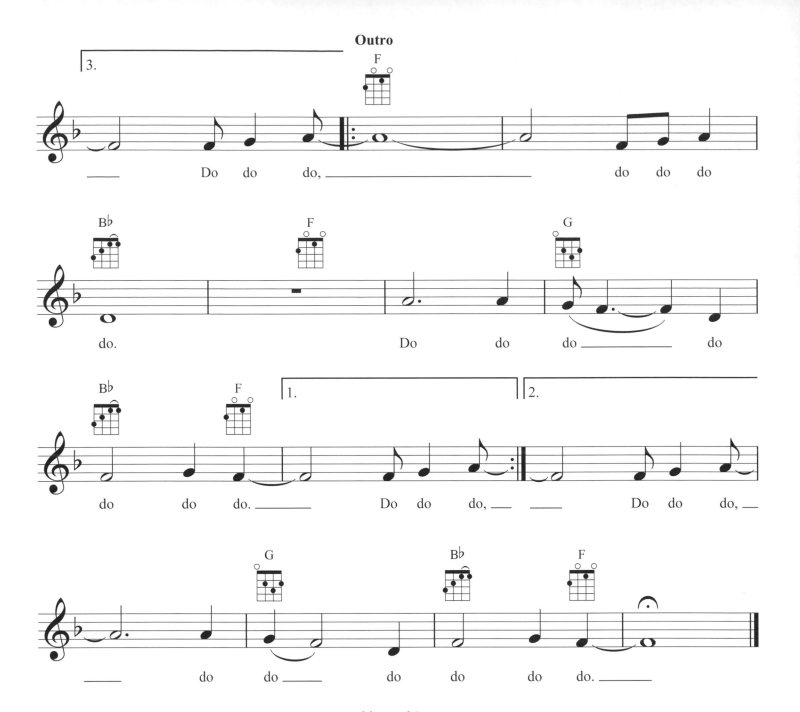

Additional Lyrics

2. River gonna take me, sing me sweet and sleepy,
   Sing me sweet and sleepy all the way back home.
   It's a far gone lullaby that I sung many years ago.
   Mama, Mama, many worlds I've come since I first left home.

Chorus: Goin' home, goin' home,
   By the waterside I will rest my bones.
   Listen to the river sing sweet songs
   To rock my soul.

3. Goin' to plant a weeping willow.
   On the bank's green edge it will grow, grow, grow.
   Sing a lullaby beside the water.
   Lovers come and go; the river roll, roll, roll.

Chorus: Fare you well, fare you well.
   I love you more than words can tell.
   Listen to the river sing sweet songs
   To rock my soul.

Candyman

Words by Robert Hunter
Music by Jerry Garcia

Copyright © 1970 ICE NINE PUBLISHING CO., INC.
Copyright Renewed
All Rights Administered by UNIVERSAL MUSIC CORP.
All Rights Reserved   Used by Permission

lay it on ____ the ___ line.   Hand me   my   old   gui - tar,

pass   the   whis - key   'round. _   Won't   you   tell ____   ev - 'ry -

bod - y   you   meet _____   that   the   Can - dy-man's   in   town? _____

Coda

D.S. al Coda

round _____   a - gain. ____

Outro-Chorus

____   Look   out,   look   out;   the   Can - dy - man, __

Repeat and fade

here   he   come   and   he's   gone _____   a - gain. __

21

Casey Jones

Words by Robert Hunter
Music by Jerry Garcia

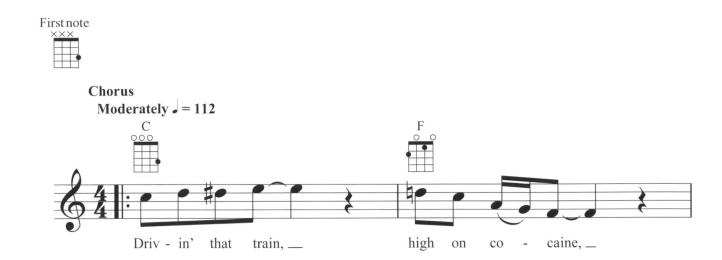

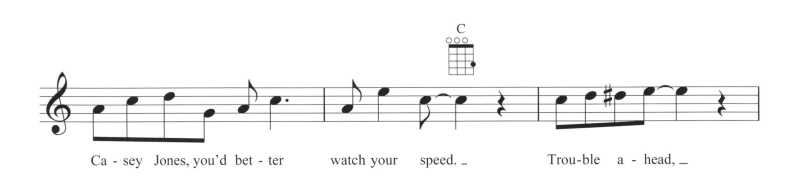

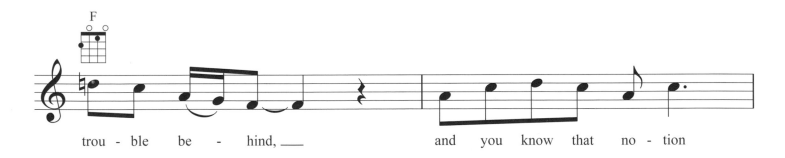

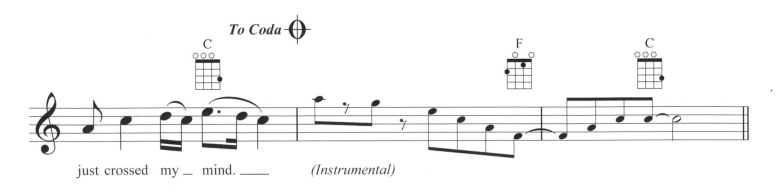

Copyright © 1970 ICE NINE PUBLISHING CO., INC.
Copyright Renewed
All Rights Administered by UNIVERSAL MUSIC CORP.
All Rights Reserved   Used by Permission

Additional Lyrics

2. Trouble ahead, the lady in red.
   Take my advice: you'd be better off dead.
   Switchman's sleeping, train hundred and two
   Is on the wrong track and headed for you.

3. Trouble with you is the trouble with me.
   Got two good eyes, but we still don't see.
   Come 'round the bend, you know it's the end.
   The fireman screams and the engine just gleams.

Dire Wolf

Words by Robert Hunter
Music by Jerry Garcia

First note

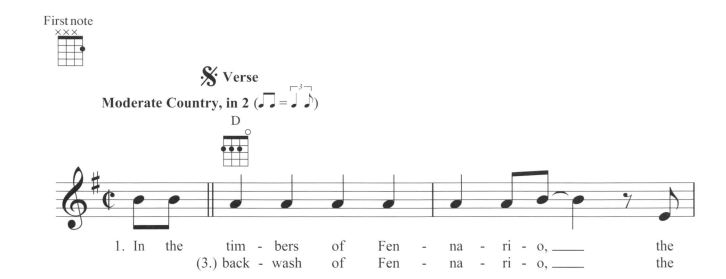

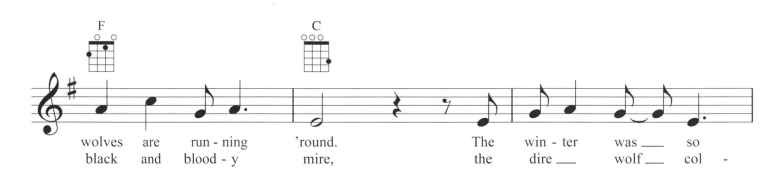

1. In the tim - bers of Fen - na - ri - o, ____ the
(3.) back - wash of Fen - na - ri - o, ____ the

wolves are run - ning 'round. The win - ter was __ so
black and blood - y mire, the dire __ wolf __ col -

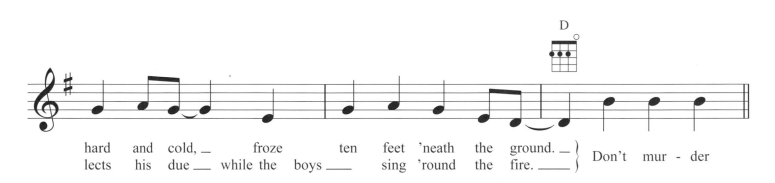

hard and cold, _ froze ten feet 'neath the ground. _ Don't mur - der
lects his due _ while the boys __ sing 'round the fire. __

Chorus

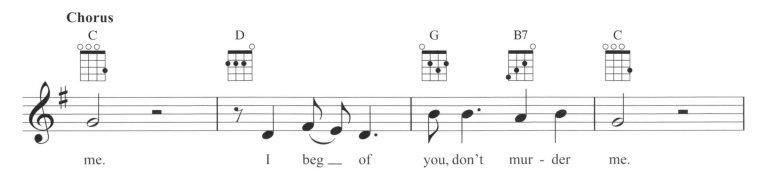

me.   I beg _ of you, don't mur - der me.

Copyright © 1970 ICE NINE PUBLISHING CO., INC.
Copyright Renewed
All Rights Administered by UNIVERSAL MUSIC CORP.
All Rights Reserved   Used by Permission

To Coda ⊕

D · C · G

Please, _____ don't mur-der me. 2. I

Verse

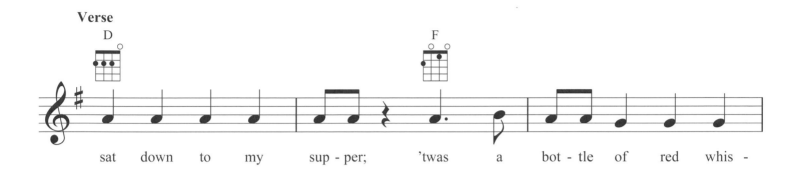

D · F

sat down to my sup-per; 'twas a bot-tle of red whis -

C

key. I said my prayers __ and went to bed; __ that's the

Chorus

G · G♭ · F · Em · D · C

last they saw of me. Don't mur-der me. I beg __ of

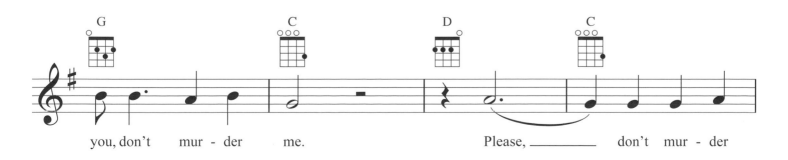

G · C · D · C

you, don't mur-der me. Please, _____ don't mur-der

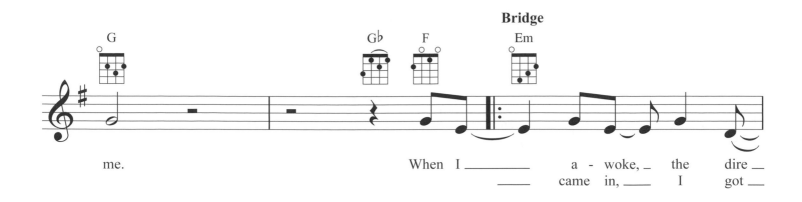

Bridge

me. When I _____ a - woke, _____ the dire _____
_____ came in, _____ I got _____

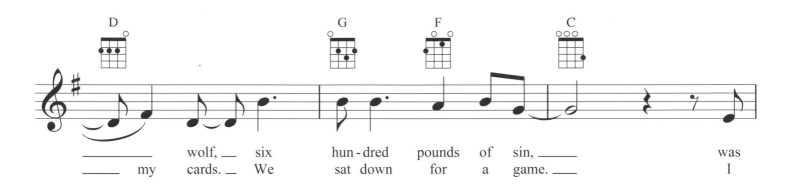

_____ wolf, _____ six hun-dred pounds of sin, _____ was
_____ my cards. _____ We sat down for a game. _____ I

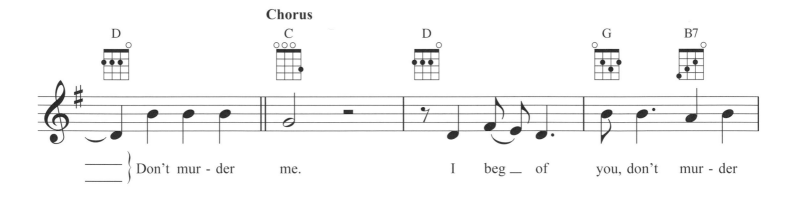

grin-ning at _____ my win - dow. All I said _____ was, "Come on in." _____
cut my deck _____ to the queen _____ of spades, but the cards were all the same. _____

Chorus

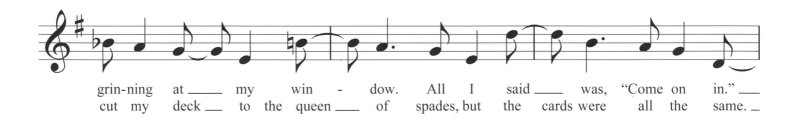

_____ Don't mur - der me. I beg _____ of you, don't mur - der

me. Please, _____ don't mur - der me.

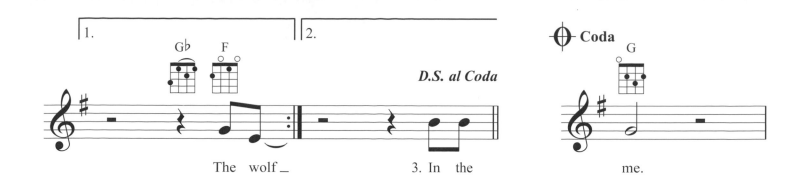

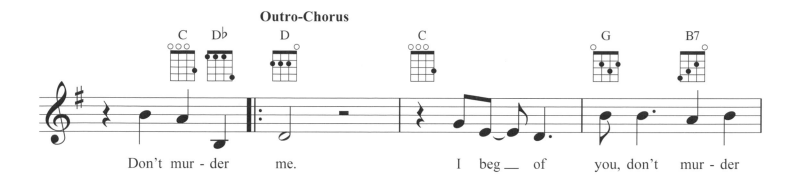

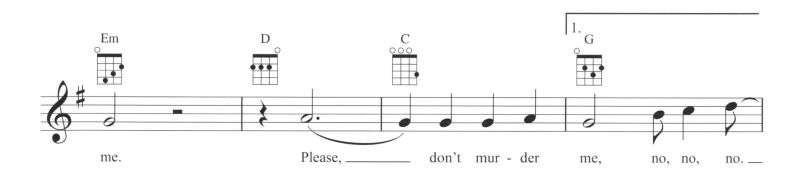

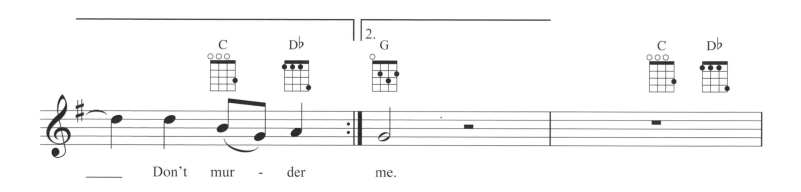

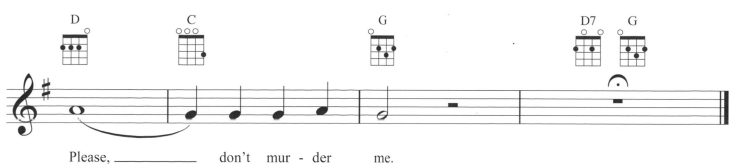

Franklin's Tower

Words by Robert Hunter
Music by Jerry Garcia and Bill Kreutzmann

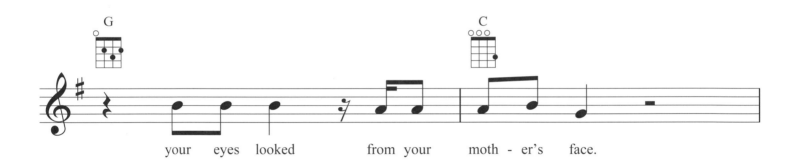

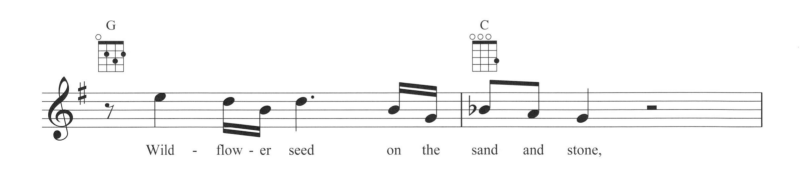

Copyright © 1975 ICE NINE PUBLISHING CO., INC.
Copyright Renewed
All Rights Administered by UNIVERSAL MUSIC CORP.
All Rights Reserved   Used by Permission

Chorus

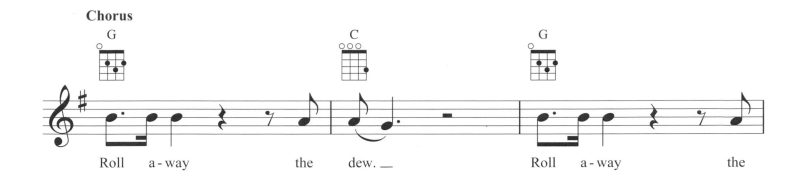

Roll a-way the dew. __ Roll a-way the

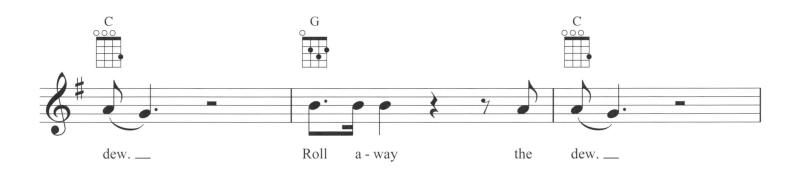

dew. __ Roll a-way the dew. __

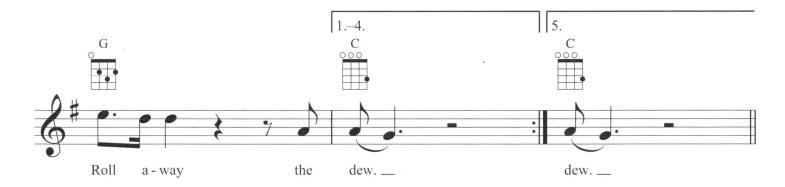

1.–4.   5.

Roll a-way the dew. __ dew. __

Outro-Chorus

Repeat and fade

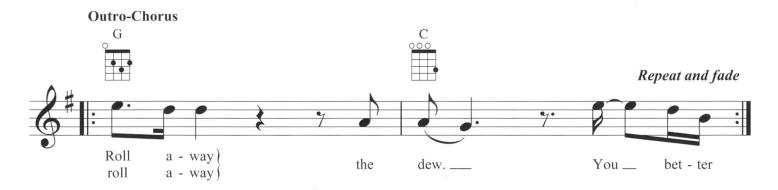

Roll a-way
roll a-way   the dew. __ You __ bet-ter

Additional Lyrics

2. I'll tell you where the four winds dwell:
   In Franklin's Tow'r there hangs a bell.
   It can ring, turn night to day;
   It can ring like fire when you lose your way.

3. God save the child who rings that bell.
   It may have one good ring, baby; you can't tell.
   One watch by night, one watch by day;
   If you get confused, listen to the music play.

4. Some come to laugh their past away,
   Some come to make it just one more day.
   Whichever way your pleasure tends,
   If you plant ice, you're gonna harvest wind.

5. In Franklin's Tow'r the four winds sleep
   Like four lean hounds the lighthouse keep.
   Wildflower seed in the sand and wind,
   May the four winds blow you home again.

Friend of the Devil

Words by Robert Hunter
Music by Jerry Garcia and John Dawson

Copyright © 1970 ICE NINE PUBLISHING CO., INC.
Copyright Renewed
All Rights Administered by UNIVERSAL MUSIC CORP.
All Rights Reserved   Used by Permission

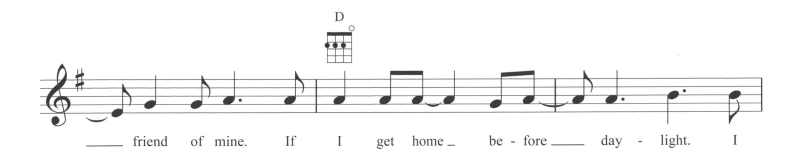

friend of mine. If I get home __ be - fore __ day - light. I

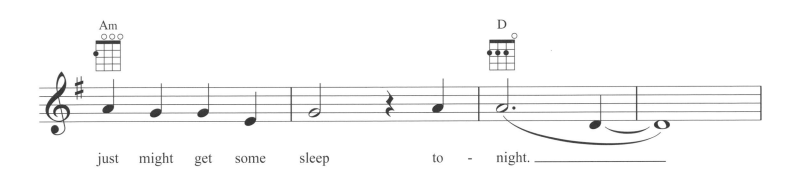

just might get some sleep to - night. _____

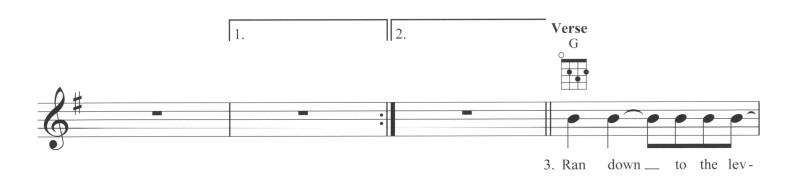

3. Ran down __ to the lev -

- ee, but __ the dev - il caught me there. __ He

took my twen - ty dol - lar bill __ and he van - ished in the air. _

%: Chorus

D

Set out run - nin', but I take my time. A

Am   D

friend of the dev - il is a friend of mine. If I get home be - fore

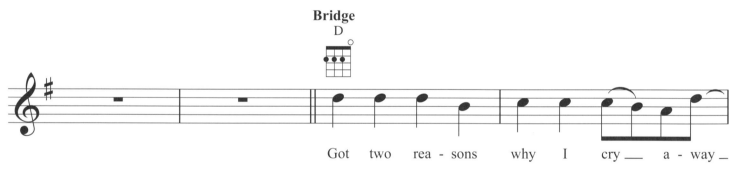

Am   To Coda ⊕ D

day - light, I just might get some sleep to - night.

Bridge

D

Got two rea - sons why I cry a - way

C

each lone - ly night. The first one's named sweet

Anne Ma - rie, and she's my heart's de - light.

Sec - ond one ___ is pris - on, ba - by; the sher - iff's on ___ my

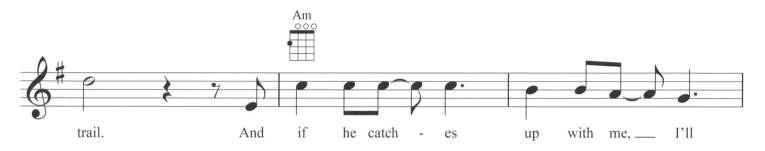

trail. And if he catch - es up with me, ___ I'll

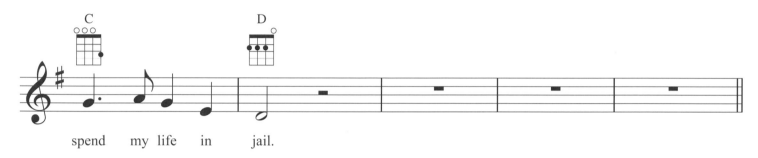

spend my life in jail.

Verse

4. Got a wife ___ in Chi - no, babe, ___ and one ___ in Cher - o - kee. ___

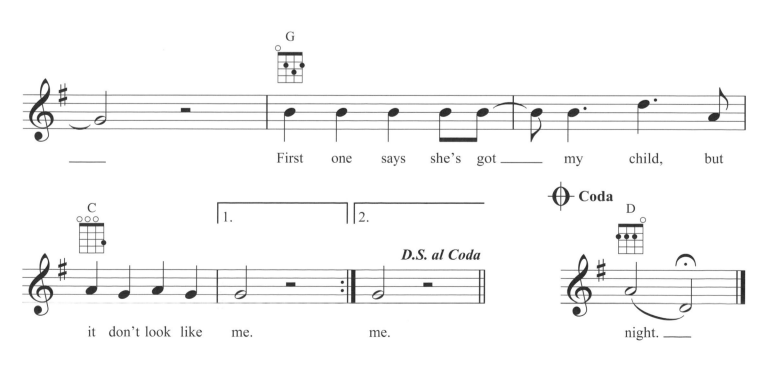

___ First one says she's got ___ my child, but

D.S. al Coda

① **Coda**

it don't look like me. me. night. ___

The Golden Road

**Words and Music by Jerry Garcia, Bill Kreutzmann,
Phil Lesh, Ron McKernan and Bob Weir**

Copyright © 1968 ICE NINE PUBLISHING CO., INC.
Copyright Renewed
All Rights Administered by UNIVERSAL MUSIC CORP.
All Rights Reserved   Used by Permission

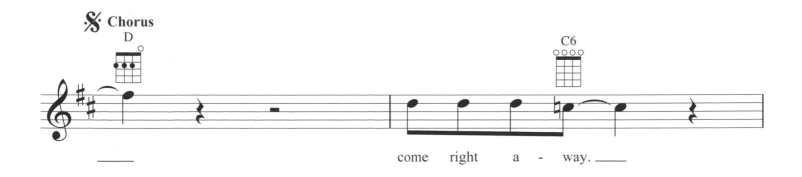

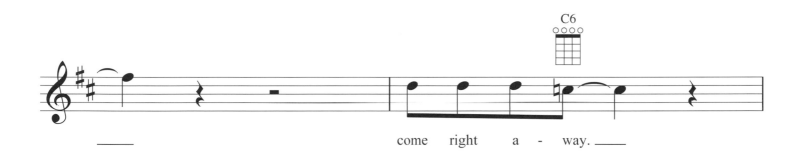

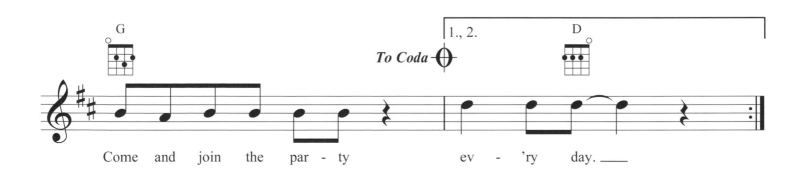

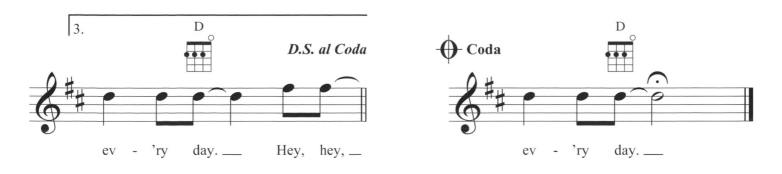

High Time

Words by Robert Hunter
Music by Jerry Garcia

Copyright © 1970 ICE NINE PUBLISHING CO., INC.
Copyright Renewed
All Rights Administered by UNIVERSAL MUSIC CORP.
All Rights Reserved   Used by Permission

living the good life. _____ Ah, _____

_____ well, ____ I _____ know.

1., 3.

2. The
4. _____

Bridge

I was los - ing time. I had

noth - ing to do, no one _____ to fight. I

came ___ to you. Wheels broke down, the

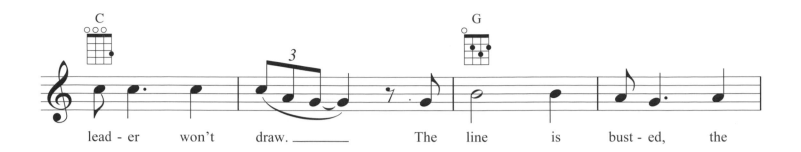

lead - er won't draw. _____ The line is bust - ed, the

last one I saw.

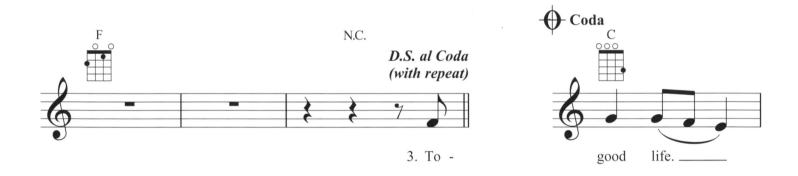

D.S. al Coda
(with repeat)

3. To -   good   life. _____

Ah, _____   well, ____ I _____ know.

Additional Lyrics

2. The wheels are muddy,
   Got a ton of hay.
   Now, listen here, baby,
   'Cause I mean what I say.
   I'm having a hard time
   Living the good life.
   Ah, well, I know.

3. Tomorrow come trouble,
   Tomorrow come pain.
   Now, don't think too hard, baby,
   'Cause you know what I'm saying.
   I could show you a high time,
   Living the good life.
   Ah, don't be that way.

4. Nothing's for certain;
   It could always go wrong.
   Come in when it's raining,
   Go on out when it's gone.
   We could have us a high time,
   Living the good life.
   Ah, well, I know.

Fire on the Mountain

Words by Robert Hunter
Music by Mickey Hart

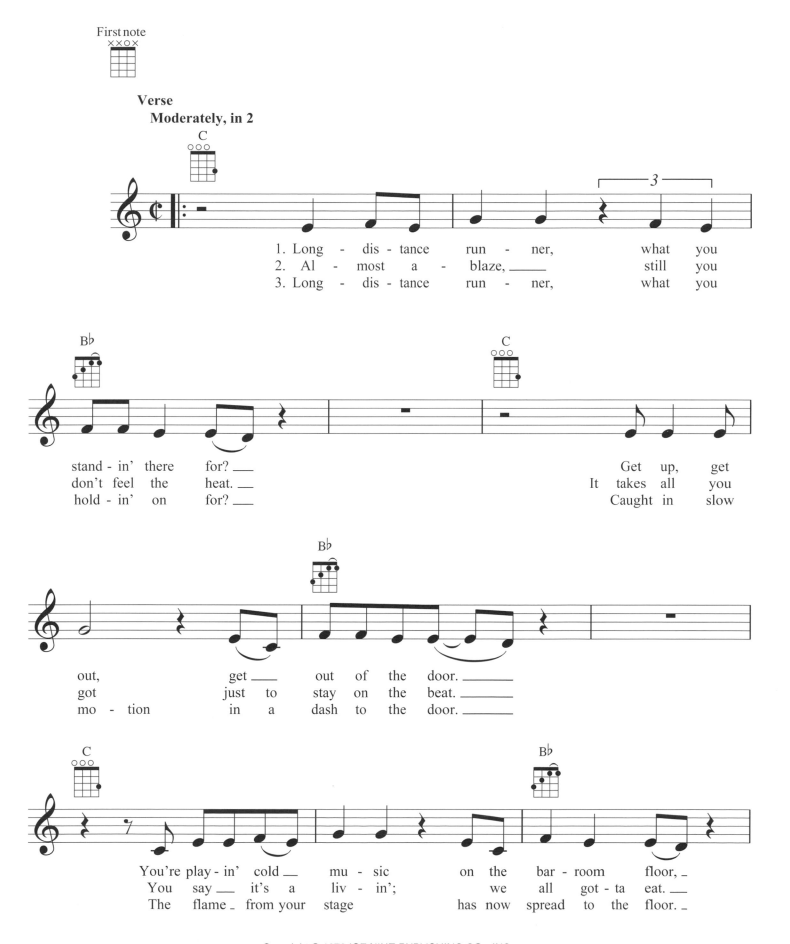

Copyright © 1978 ICE NINE PUBLISHING CO., INC.
All Rights Administered by UNIVERSAL MUSIC CORP.
All Rights Reserved   Used by Permission

drowned in your laugh - ter and
But you're here a - lone; there's no
You gave all you had; why you

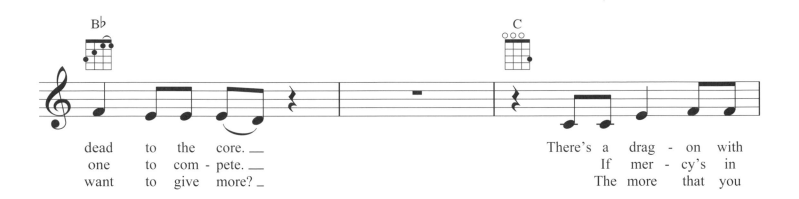

dead to the core. ___
one to com - pete. ___ There's a drag - on with
want to give more? _ If mer - cy's in
The more that you

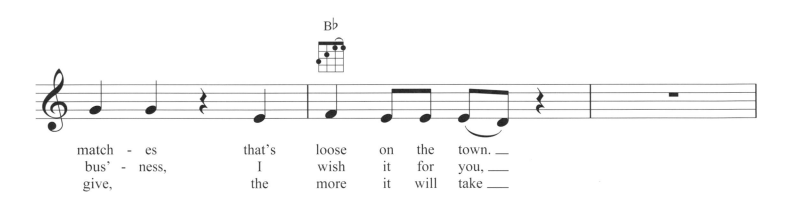

match - es that's loose on the town. ___
bus' - ness, I wish it for you, ___
give, the more it will take ___

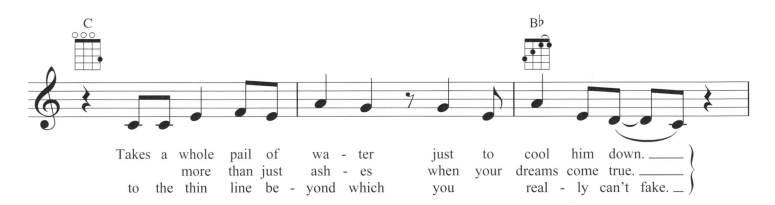

Takes a whole pail of wa - ter just to cool him down. _____
more than just ash - es when your dreams come true. _____
to the thin line be - yond which you real - ly can't fake. _

Chorus

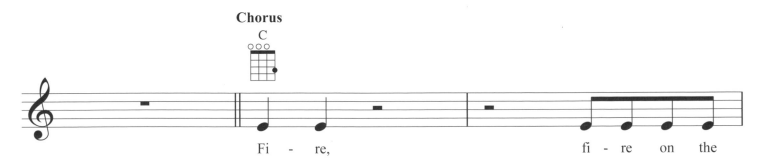

Fi - re, fi - re on the

40

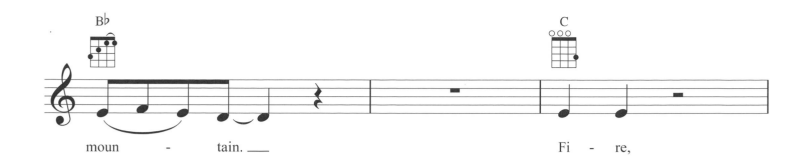

moun - tain. ___ Fi - re,

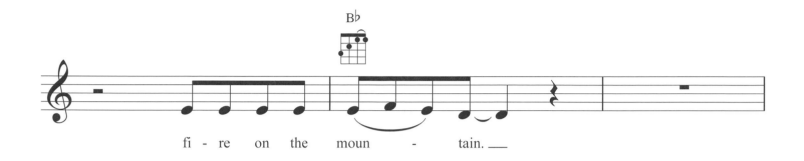

fi - re on the moun - tain. ___

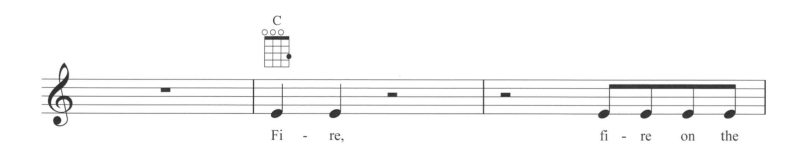

Fi - re, fi - re on the moun - tain. ___

Fi - re, fi - re on the

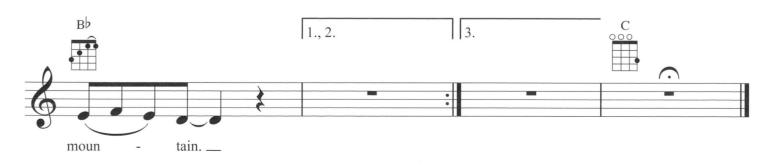

1., 2.   3.

moun - tain. ___

Ripple

Words by Robert Hunter
Music by Jerry Garcia

First note

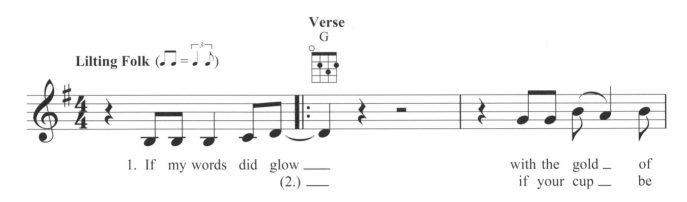

Copyright © 1971 ICE NINE PUBLISHING CO., INC.
Copyright Renewed
All Rights Administered by UNIVERSAL MUSIC CORP.
All Rights Reserved   Used by Permission

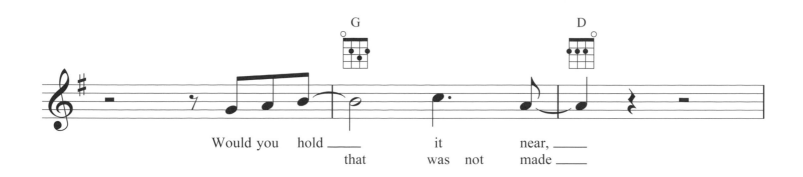

Would you hold ___ it near, ___
that was not made ___

as it were ___ your own? ___ It's a hand - me - down, ___
by the hands ___ of men. ___ There ___ is a road, ___

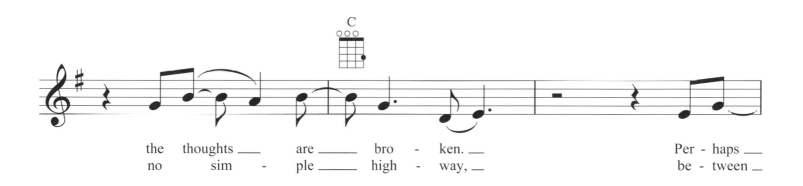

the thoughts ___ are ___ bro - ken. ___ Per - haps ___
no sim - ple ___ high - way, ___ be - tween ___

___ they're bet -ter left un - sung. I don't know, ___
___ the dawn and the dark ___ of night. And if you

___ don't real - ly care. ___
go, no one ___ may fol - low. ___

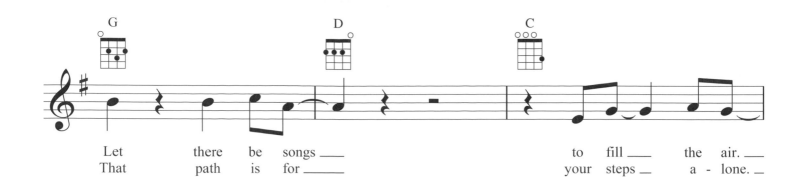

Let there be songs ___ to fill ___ the air. ___
That path is for ___ your steps ___ a - lone. ___

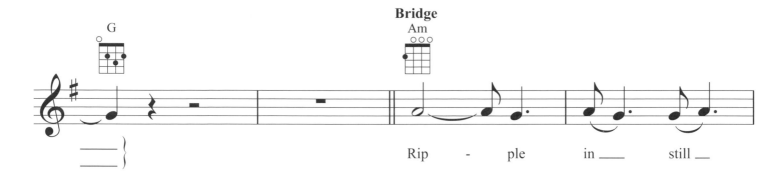

Bridge

___ } Rip - ple in ___ still ___

wa - ter, ___ when there is ___ no peb - ble tossed, ___

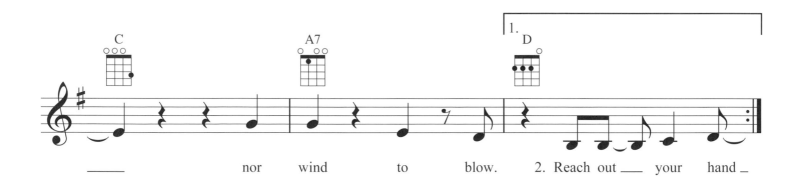

1.

___ nor wind to blow. 2. Reach out ___ your hand ___

2. **Verse**

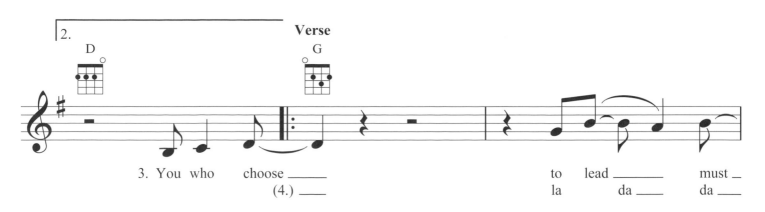

3. You who choose ___ to lead ___ must ___
(4.) ___ la da ___ da ___

_____ fol - low. _____ But if _____ you
_____ da da, _____ da da _____ da

fall, you fall a - lone. _____ If you should stand, _
da da da da da. _____ La da da da, _

_____ then who's _ to guide you? _
_____ da da _____ da da da, _____

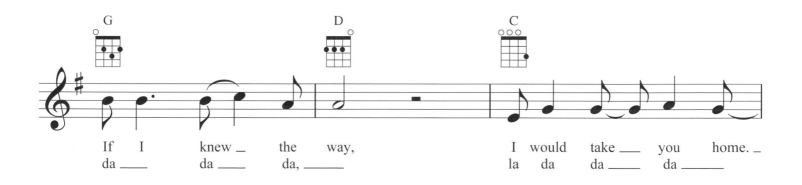

If I knew _ the way, I would take _ you home. _
da _____ da _____ da, _____ la da da _____ da _____

1.
_____ 4. La dee da da da, _____ da.

2.

Rosemary

Words by Robert Hunter
Music by Jerry Garcia

Copyright © 1969 ICE NINE PUBLISHING CO., INC.
Copyright Renewed
All Rights Administered by UNIVERSAL MUSIC CORP.
All Rights Reserved   Used by Permission

Ramble On Rose

Words by Robert Hunter
Music by Jerry Garcia

Copyright © 1972 ICE NINE PUBLISHING CO., INC.
Copyright Renewed
All Rights Administered by UNIVERSAL MUSIC CORP.
All Rights Reserved   Used by Permission

_____ er,
pace the halls ___ and climb the walls ___
"One go up ___ and one come down. ___
clank your chains ___ and count your change ___

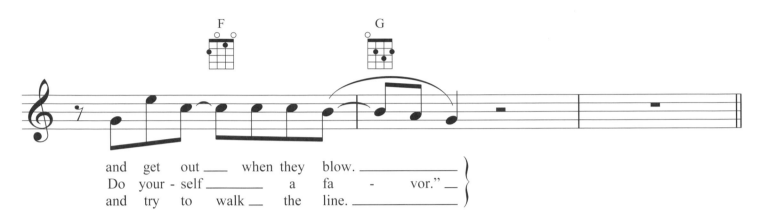

and get out ___ when they blow. _____
Do your - self _____ a fa - vor." ___
and try to walk ___ the line. _____

Chorus

Did you say ___ your name ___ was Ram - bl - in' Rose? ___

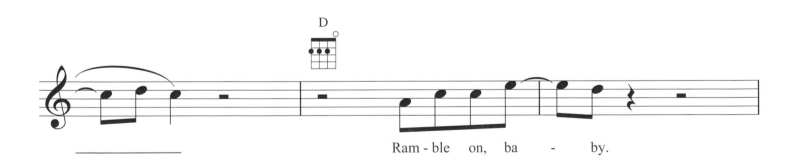

_____ Ram - ble on, ba - by.

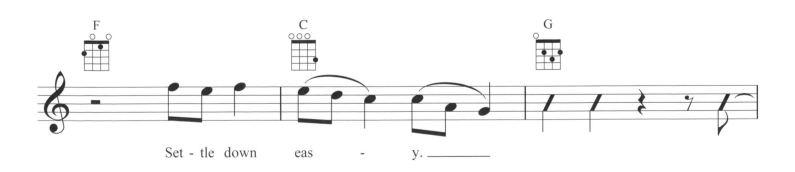

Set - tle down eas - y. _____

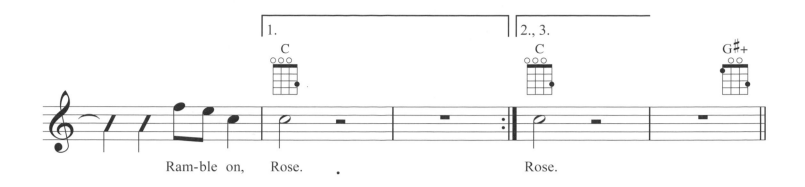

Ram-ble on, Rose. Rose.

Bridge

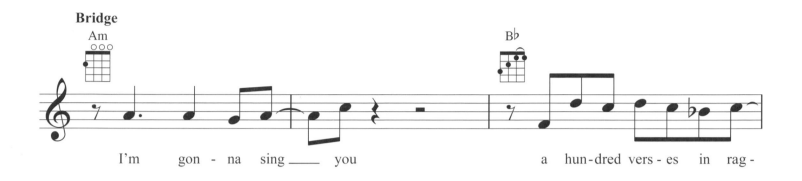

I'm gon-na sing ___ you a hun-dred vers-es in rag-

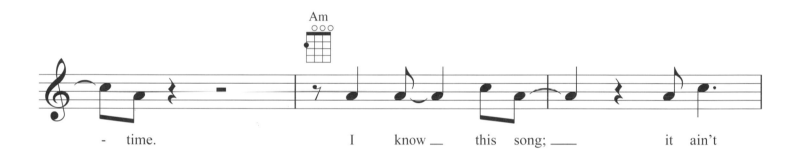

- time. I know ___ this song; ___ it ain't

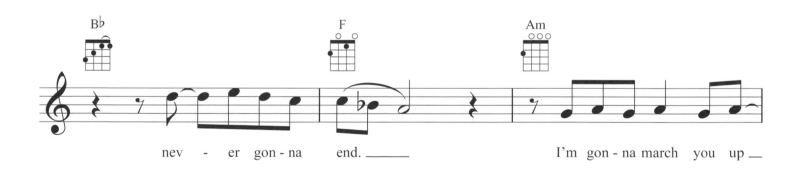

nev - er gon-na end. _____ I'm gon-na march you up ___

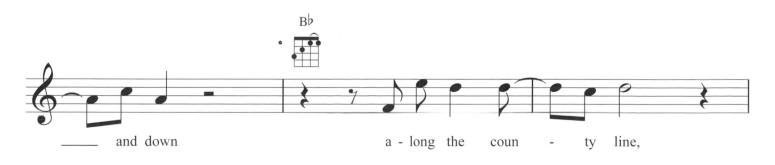

_____ and down a - long the coun - ty line,

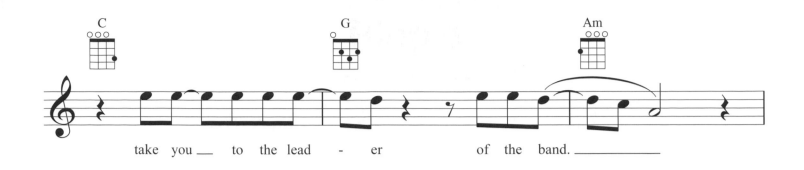

take you __ to the lead - er   of the band. _____

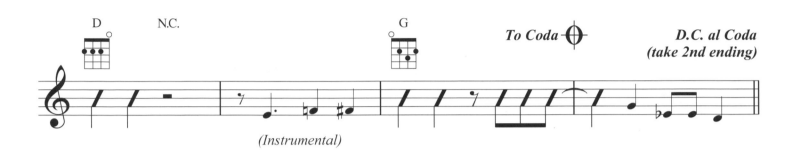

(Instrumental)

(Instrumental)   4. Good-bye,   Ma-ma and Pa - pa.

Good-bye,   Jack   and Jill. _____   The   grass ain't green - er,   the

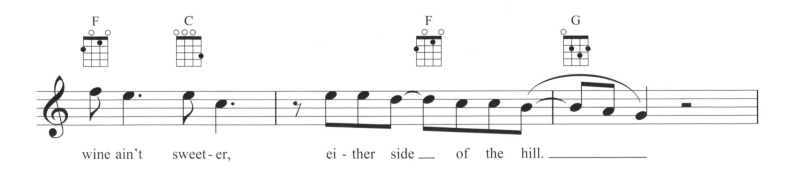

wine ain't sweet-er,   ei - ther side __ of the hill. _____

Chorus

But _____ did you say _____ your name _ was

Ram - bl - in' Rose? _____ Ram - ble on, ba -

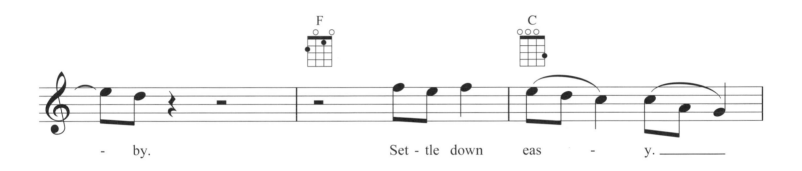

- by. Set - tle down eas - y. _____

Ram - ble on, Rose.

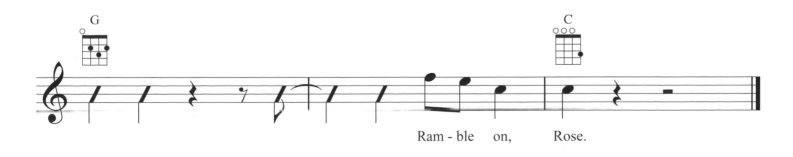

Ram - ble on, Rose.

Scarlet Begonias

Words by Robert Hunter
Music by Jerry Garcia

Copyright © 1974 ICE NINE PUBLISHING CO., INC.
Copyright Renewed
All Rights Administered by UNIVERSAL MUSIC CORP.
All Rights Reserved   Used by Permission

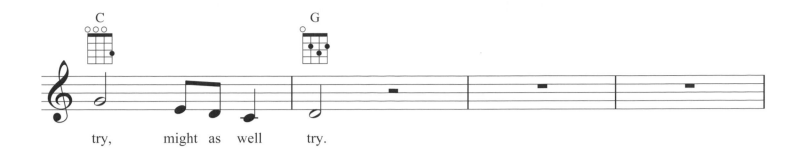

try,   might as well   try.

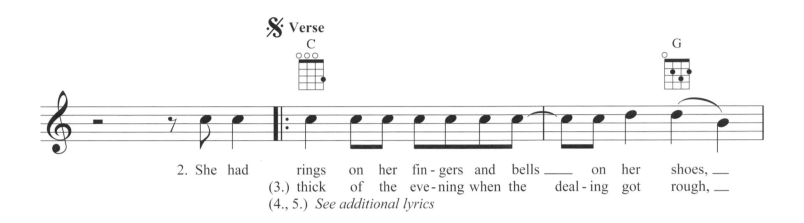

%. Verse

2. She had   rings on her fin - gers and bells ___ on her   shoes, ___
(3.) thick   of the eve - ning when the deal - ing got   rough, ___
(4., 5.) *See additional lyrics*

and I knew ___ with - out ask - in' she was
she was too ___ pat to o - pen and ___

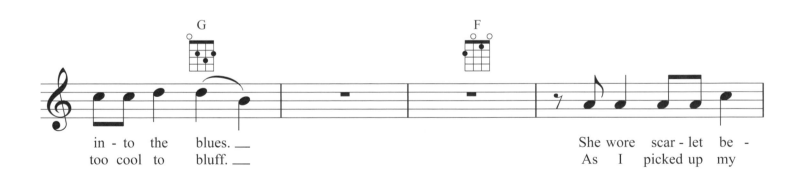

in - to the   blues. ___   She wore scar - let be -
too cool to   bluff. ___   As I picked up my

go -   nias   tucked in - to her   curls.
match - es   and was clos - ing the   door,

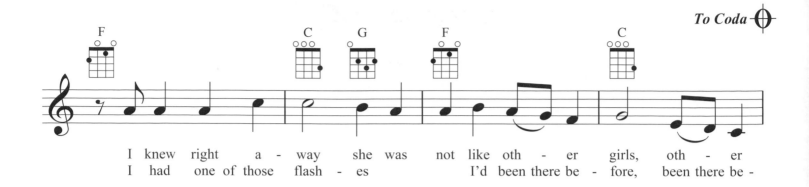

I knew right a - way she was not like oth - er girls, oth - er
I had one of those flash - es I'd been there be - fore, been there be -

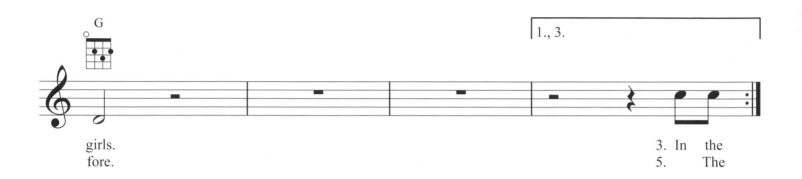

girls.   3. In the
fore.   5. The

Bridge

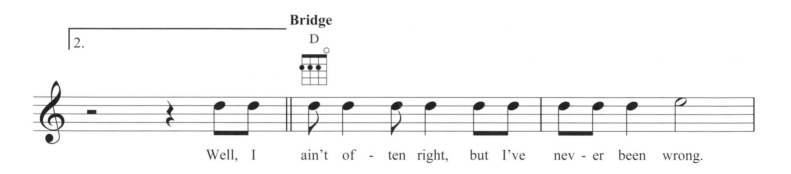

Well, I ain't of - ten right, but I've nev - er been wrong.

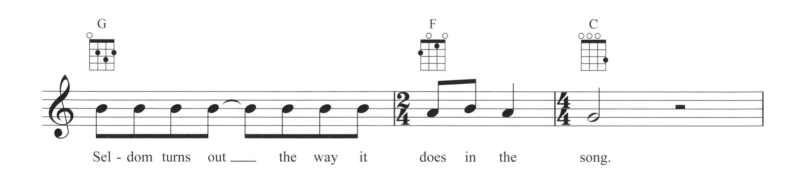

Sel - dom turns out ___ the way it does in the song.

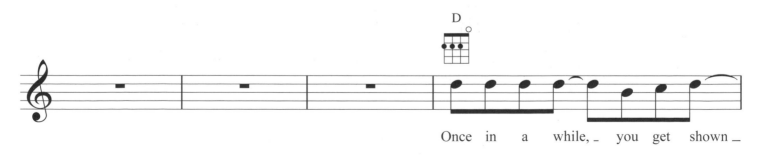

Once in a while, _ you get shown _

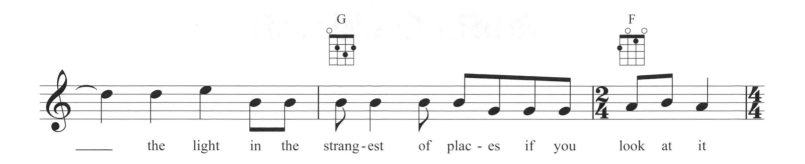

the light in the strang-est of plac-es if you look at it

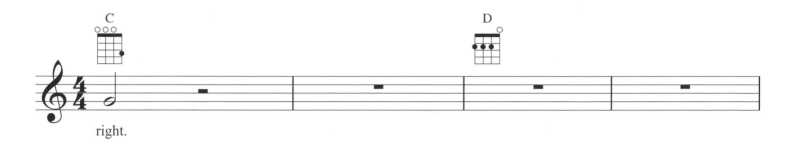

right.

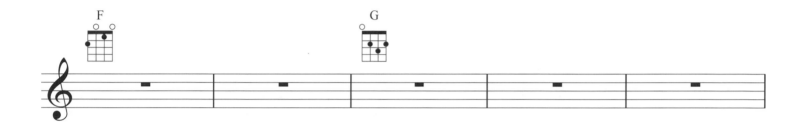

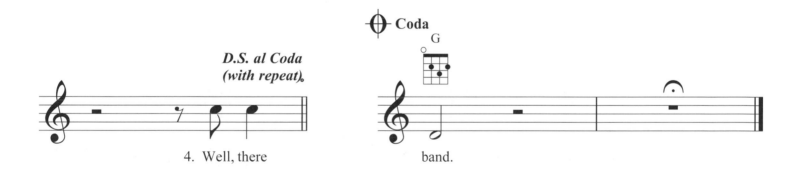

D.S. al Coda (with repeat).

4. Well, there

Coda

band.

Additional Lyrics

4. Well, there ain't nothin' wrong with the way she moves,
   Or scarlet begonias or a touch of the blues.
   And there's nothin' wrong with the look that's in her eye.
   I had to learn the hard way to let her pass by,
   Let her pass by.

5. The wind in the willows playin' "Tea for Two,"
   The sky was yellow and the sun was blue.
   Strangers stoppin' strangers just to shake their hand.
   Ev'rybody is playing in the heart of gold band,
   Heart of gold band.

Sugar Magnolia

Words by Robert Hunter
Music by Bob Weir

Copyright © 1970 ICE NINE PUBLISHING CO., INC.
Copyright Renewed
All Rights Administered by UNIVERSAL MUSIC CORP.
All Rights Reserved   Used by Permission

We can dis - cov - er the won - ders of na - ture, roll - ing in the rush - es down _____

_____ by the riv - er - side.

Chorus

She's got ev - 'ry - thing _____ de - light - ful, she's got ev - 'ry - thing _____

_____ I need. Takes the wheel _ when I'm _____ see - ing dou - ble,

pays my tick - et when I speed. _____

Verse

2. Well, she comes skim - ming through rays _____ of vio - let;

-mer night moon - light, cra - zy in the sun - light, yes, in - deed.

Verse

3. Some - times __ when the cuck -

- oo's cry - ing, when the moon __ is half - way down,

some - times __ when the night ___ is dy - ing, I take me out __ and I

wan - der a - round, _____ I wan - der 'round. __

Outro

The sun - shine __ day - dream. ___

Walk-ing in the tall ___ trees. _____

Go - ing where the wind goes. _____ Bloom-ing like a

red ___ rose. Breath-ing more ___ free - ly. _____

Ride out sing - ing; I'll walk ___ you in the morn - ing sun - shine. ___

Sun - shine ___ day - dream. ___ (Do do do,

Repeat and fade

do do ___ do do, do do do, do _____ do do do.)

Touch of Grey

Words by Robert Hunter
Music by Jerry Garcia

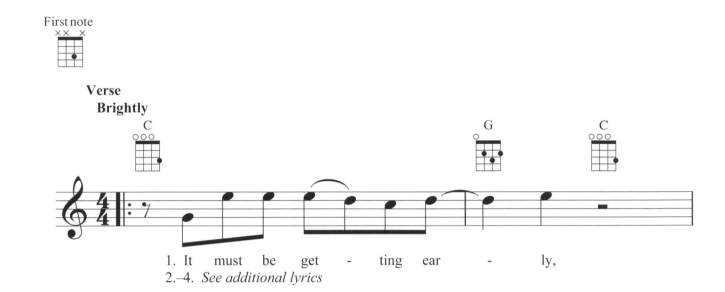

First note

Verse
Brightly

1. It must be get - ting ear - ly,
2.–4. *See additional lyrics*

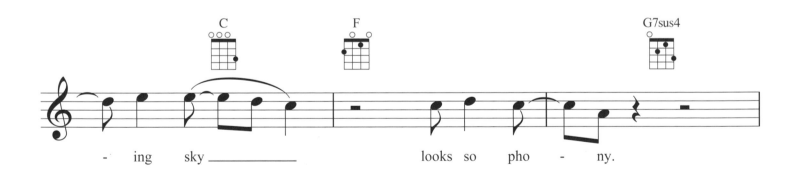

clocks are run - ning late. ____ Paint - by - num - ber morn -

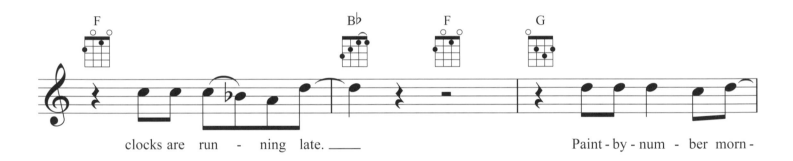

- ing sky _____ looks so pho - ny.

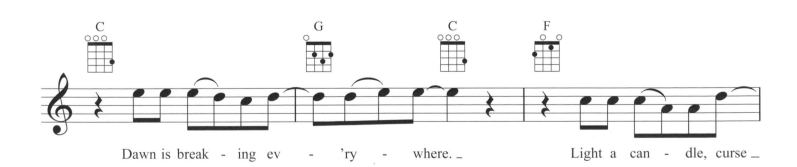

Dawn is break - ing ev - 'ry - where. _ Light a can - dle, curse _

Copyright © 1987 ICE NINE PUBLISHING CO., INC.
All Rights Administered by UNIVERSAL MUSIC CORP.
All Rights Reserved   Used by Permission

Outro-Chorus

(Instrumental) We will get by. _____

We will get by. _____

We will get by. _____ We will __ sur - vive. _

Repeat and fade

Additional Lyrics

2. I see you've got your list out; say your piece and get out.
   Yes, I get the gist of it, but it's alright.
   Sorry that you feel that way. The only thing there is to say:
   Ev'ry silver lining's got a touch of grey.

3. I know the rent is in arrears, the dog has not been fed in years.
   It's even worse than it appears, but it's alright.
   Cows giving kerosene, kid can't read at seventeen.
   The words he knows are all obscene, but it's alright.

4. The shoe is on the hand it fits, there's really nothing much to it.
   Whistle through your teeth and spit 'cause it's alright.
   Oh, well, a touch of grey, kinda suits you anyway.
   That was all I had to say, and it's alright.

Uncle John's Band

Words by Robert Hunter
Music by Jerry Garcia

Copyright © 1970 ICE NINE PUBLISHING CO., INC.
Copyright Renewed
All Rights Administered by UNIVERSAL MUSIC CORP.
All Rights Reserved   Used by Permission

come   to take   his chil - dren   home. ___

Verse

3. It's ___ the same sto - ry   the   crow told me, ___ it's the
4. I   live   in   a   sil - ver mine ___ and   I

on - ly one ___ he   knows.   Like   the   morn - ing ___
call   it   Beg - gar's   Tomb.   I   got ___ me   a

sun   you come ___ and ___ like   the   wind ___ you   go.
vi - o - lin ___ and   I   beg   you   call ___ the   tune.

Ain't   no   time ___ to   hate, ___   bare - ly   time ___ to   wait. ___
An - y - bod - y's   choice, ___   I   can   hear ___ your   voice. ___

___   Whoa,   oh, ___ what   I   want ___ to   know: ___
___   Whoa,   oh, ___ what   I   want ___ to   know: ___

_____ where _ does _ the time go?
_____ how _ does _ the song go?

Chorus

Come hear Un - cle John's Band by the riv - er - side. _____
Come hear Un - cle John's Band play - ing to the tide. _____

_____ Got some things to talk _____ a - bout _____
_____ Come on a - long or go _____ a - lone, _____ he's

1.
2.

here be - side the _ ris - ing tide. _____
come to take his _ chil - - dren home.

Outro

Da da da da da da. Da da da da da

da. Da da da da da da.

Truckin'

Words by Robert Hunter
Music by Jerry Garcia, Phil Lesh and Bob Weir

First note

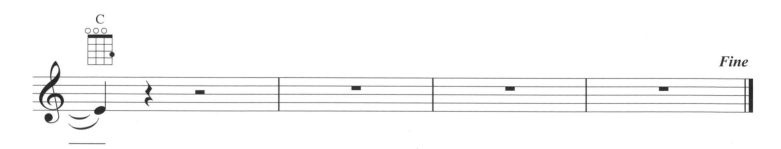

Copyright © 1971 ICE NINE PUBLISHING CO., INC.
Copyright Renewed
All Rights Administered by UNIVERSAL MUSIC CORP.
All Rights Reserved   Used by Permission

Verse

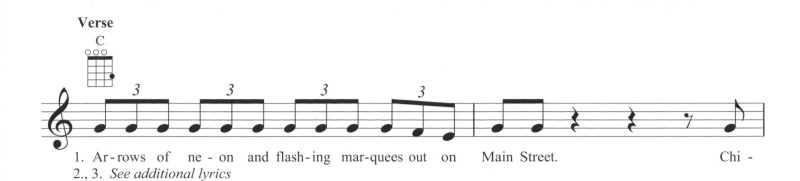

1. Ar-rows of ne - on and flash-ing mar-quees out on   Main Street.   Chi -
2., 3. *See additional lyrics*

ca - go, New York, De - troit and it's all   on   the   same street.   Your

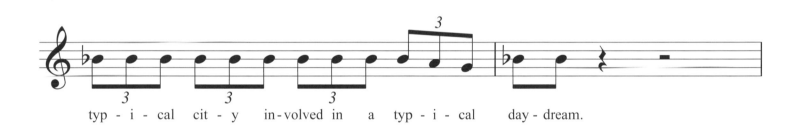

typ - i - cal cit - y in-volved in   a   typ - i - cal   day - dream.

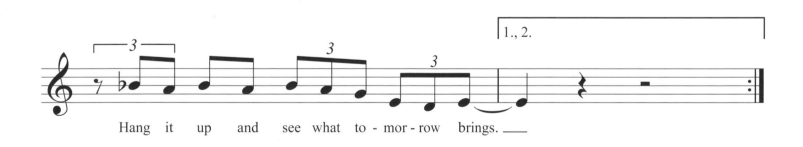

Hang   it   up   and   see what to - mor - row   brings. ___

Bridge

___   Some-times   the light's   all   shin - ing   on   me.

Oth - er times — I can bare - ly see.

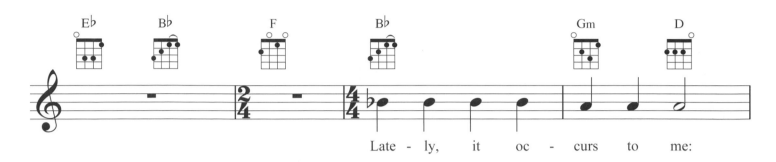

Late - ly, it oc - curs to me:

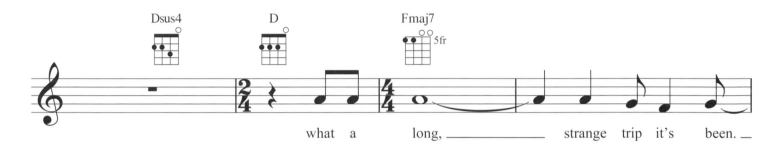

what a long, _____ strange trip it's been. _

D.C. al Fine

Additional Lyrics

Chorus 2: Dallas got a soft machine. Houston, too close to New Orleans.
New York got the ways and means, but just won't let you be.

Verse 2: What in the world ever became of sweet Jane?
She lost her sparkle; you know, she isn't the same.
Living on reds, vitamin C and cocaine,
All a friend can say is, "Ain't it a shame?"

Chorus 3: Truckin' up to Buffalo. Been thinking, you got to mellow slow.
Takes time, you pick a place to go, and just keep truckin' on.

Verse 3: You're sick of hangin' around, you'd like to travel.
Get tired of travelin', you want to settle down.
I guess they can't revoke your soul for tryin'.
Get out of the door, light out and look all around.

Chorus 4: Truckin', I'm a-going home, whoa, whoa, baby, back where I belong.
Back home, sit down and patch my bones, and get back truckin' on.